Flowers, Gemstones & Jesus:

Finding Jesus in the Months of the Year

Carol Peterson

Honor Bound Books

Honor Bound Books

Copyright by Carol Peterson, 2016

All rights reserved. No portion of this book may be reproduced, stored in a retrieval system, or transmitted in any form or by any means—electronic, mechanical, photocopy, recording, scanning, or other—except for brief quotations in critical reviews or articles, without the prior written permission of the publisher.

Unless otherwise noted, all scripture quotations are taken from *The Holy Bible*, New International Version (NIV). Copyright © Biblica. Used with permission. All rights reserved.

Interior graphic Ornament 1 used with permission from Adobe. Typeset in 18/24 Papyrus, 14 pt Viner Hand and 12/16/20 pt Cambria, used with permission from Microsoft.

Dedication

This book is dedicated to my readers who have encouraged me to continue to see Jesus in the world around us and then share those parables with others.

Flowers, Gemstones & Jesus

Finding Jesus

in the Months of the Year

Contents

Our Days are Numbered 1

A Year Divided by Twelve 7

January: Carnations, Garnets & the Christ Child 9

February: Irises, Violets, Amethyst & Valentines 17

March: Daffodils, Aquamarine & Lent 25

April: Sweet Peas, Daisies, Diamonds & Easter 33

May: Lilies of the Valley, Emeralds & Mom 39

June: Roses, Pearls & the Gospel 47

July: Larkspurs, Lilies, Rubies & Freedom 55

August: Gladiolas, Poppies, Peridot & Priests 63

September: Asters, Glories, Sapphires & Saviors 71

October: Marigolds, Tourmaline, Opal & Saints 79

November: Chrysanthemums, Topaz, Citrine & Sonshine 87

December: Poinsettias, Blue Topaz, Tanzanite & Treasures 95

For Those Seeking Salvation 103

Keep Finding and Sharing Jesus 109

More Flowers, Gemstones, Gold & Silver in Scripture 117

Author's Thanks

Books by Carol Peterson

About the Author

Our Days are Numbered

Teach us to number our days, that we may gain a heart of wisdom (Psalm 90:12).

When we are little, we think we'll never grow up. We'll never be old enough to do what we want, when we want, how we want or with whom.

Then we become young adults and we think we're invincible. We know everything, understand everything and have all the time in the world to accomplish each and every dream we have. And then dream up more dreams.

Ultimately we reach a point in our lives when we start looking ahead and behind and wonder where the time went. What did we do with all those years God had given us?

A better question would be: What will we do with the time God still has left for us?

Our Days are Numbered

God created time for our benefit. He knew we needed a way to number our days—to keep track of the finiteness of our lives and to look forward to the days of our future.

Scripture tells us that to God, a day is like a thousand. And vice versa. He doesn't need to keep track of time. He has eternity.

We also have eternity with Him, when we call upon Jesus' name and accept His gift of salvation.

Eternity in heaven with Jesus. It'll be awesome and incomprehensible to our present human thinking. But that still leaves us with the question: what will we do with the time God has given us here on this small blue planet? How will we leave this earth better for having lived on it?

Equally important, how will we share the hope of eternity with people we love? By sharing Jesus with them. To make that easier, Jesus reveals Himself and His qualities, His love and His plan everywhere. We can see Jesus in flowers, in gemstones and in time itself. If we only look.

And then we can share those realizations with others. When we celebrate someone's birthday, we can tell them about the flower that represents their birth month. We can explain how their birthstone has qualities of Jesus. We can use the celebration of their birth to show why every day should be a celebration of the life we have in Jesus.

Our Calendar

Jesus created time for us 'way back in the beginning, when He separated the darkness from the light, giving us days and nights. Jesus didn't need the concept of time, but He knew we do. We humans went on to create calendars to keep track of those days.

Early Lunar Calendars

Early in human history, most calendars were based on the phases of the moon. Mankind, standing on planet earth, could not know that earth circled the sun. But we could see clearly that the moon had phases which repeated over time.

Those lunar-based calendars helped farmers know when to plant crops and worked well for everyday life. But when mankind began to record history, the need for a more sophisticated calendar became important. Enter Julius and Augustus Caesar.

A More Advanced Lunar Calendar

Our modern calendar is credited in part to the Roman Empire. Back in the 5th century BC, the Roman Empire was immense. And the Caesars needed to track time better in order to rule effectively and—as immense governments do—gather immense taxes from the citizens.

Our Days are Numbered

The early Julian calendar ordered by Augustus Caesar and completed during Julius Caesar's reign—was still lunar based, but also incorporated a leap year every four years which brought it closer to a more accurate solar-based calendar.

Our Solar Calendar

The Julian calendar was widely used until Copernicus, Galileo and other scientists in the 15th and 16th centuries developed the science that led to our understanding that the earth revolves around the sun. Once our place in the solar system was more clearly understood, the Roman Catholic Church commissioned the creation of a new 365-1/4 day calendar in order to find a better way to track the date on which Easter is calculated.

This Gregorian calendar, commissioned by Pope Gregory XIII in 1582 was later modified to add one day in every year divisible by four. Also, one extra day is added if the year is divisible by 400. Despite all these additional leap days added to the calendar, it remains "off" by about 26 seconds each year. That means, we'll have to add one more day in a couple thousand years.

But for now, things are close enough that we can plan our days and live them in a way that honors Jesus. Because our Gregorian calendar was a modification of the Julian Roman calendar, many of the names of the months still contain meanings from ancient Roman culture. Although the names of

Roman gods and goddesses continue to decorate our calendars, we all know and remember that it was the true God who created time in the first place.

The Calendar as a Tool of Evangelism

Everyone in this world is aware of time. We rely on time. We track time in the same way. We are conscious of the fact that we have a limited number of days to live in this world. The issue of time is a universal topic of conversation.

Regardless of our theology, our spirituality, our "religion,"—or lack thereof—one thing we have in common is an understanding and tracking of time.

Jesus' "Great Commission" commanded (not suggested; not implied; not hinted) us to go and teach others about Him and His good news of salvation.

> *"Therefore go and make disciples of all nations, baptizing them in the name of the Father and of the Son and of the Holy Spirit, and teaching them to obey everything I have commanded you. And surely I am with you always, to the very end of the age"* (Matthew 28:19-20).

Despite this command and regardless of our genuine desire to introduce Jesus to others, we are often at a loss as to how to bring up the topic in casual conversation. Often we feel we must corner someone and allot a large block of time before we can begin to start a conversation about salvation. Other times, we feel we must research our theology and have every question answered before we can bring up the subject.

We need look no further than our watch, our cell phone screen or our calendar, however for conversation starters. All of us have the commonality of time as a basis for discussion. Everyone has a birthday or knows someone with an upcoming birthday. Everyone is interested in time.

So how can we relate our common interest in the calendar to a way to introduce others to Jesus? By finding Jesus in the months of the year.

A Year Divided by Twelve

*There is a time for everything, and a season for every activity under the heavens:
a time to be born and a time to die,
a time to plant and a time to uproot,
a time to kill and a time to heal,
a time to tear down and a time to build,
a time to weep and a time to laugh,
a time to mourn and a time to dance,
a time to scatter stones and a time to gather them,
a time to embrace and a time to refrain from embracing,
a time to search and a time to give up,
a t time to keep and a time to throw away,
a time to tear and a time to mend,
a time to be silent and a time to speak,
a time to love and a time to hate,
a time for war and a time for peace.*
(Ecclesiastes 3:1-8)

January: Carnations, Garnets & the Christ Child

~

And God said, "Let there be light," and there was light. God saw that the light was good, and he separated the light from the darkness. God called the light "day," and the darkness he called "night." And there was evening, and there was morning—the first day (Genesis 1:3-5).

Let's Talk about January

The Christian church designates January 6 (twelve days after Christmas) as the date set aside to celebrate Epiphany. In everyday language use, the word *epiphany* means an illuminative discovery or realization. In the Christian calendar, Epiphany (capitalized) refers to the day the Wise Men visited the Christ child.

January

On coming to the house, they saw the child with his mother Mary, and they bowed down and worshiped him. Then they opened their treasures and presented him with gifts of gold, frankincense and myrrh (Matthew 2:11)

Bible scholars suggest the Wise Men didn't visit Jesus until He was a bit older than a newborn babe. Just as Jesus was most likely not born on a date that corresponds to our December 25, the Wise Men probably did not actually show up on January 6. Regardless of the actual "when" however, January 6 is the date on our calendars recognized as the date of the Epiphany.

The significance of the Epiphany (capitalized) is that it was that moment when the deity of Jesus was shown to the Gentiles (the Wise Men from the east who were not Jews). Jesus tells us that He came first to save the Jews. But the Epiphany reminds us that although Jesus was born into Jewish society, He came also to save the rest of the world as well. For those Wise Men of old, meeting Jesus and realizing in whose presence they were, must have indeed been an illuminative discovery.

The word January (the name of the first month in the original Roman calendar) came from the root word *Janus*. In Roman mythology, Janus was the Roman god of doorways and gates. He is often depicted visually as having two faces, each facing a different direction. Such a visual image reminds us that January is the first month of the New Year. Thus we can look back on the old and forward to what is to come.

January

Jesus also is the God of gates. In fact Scripture tells us that Jesus is the narrow gate; that none shall enter heaven except through Him.

> *"Enter through the narrow gate. For wide is the gate and broad is the road that leads to destruction, and many enter through it. But small is the gate and narrow the road that leads to life, and only a few find it"* (Matthew 7:13-14).

In other words, if the month of January was named after the Roman god of gates, it will be easy to think of that word meaning and remember Jesus—the only gate that matters.

Carnations

The flower that represents the month of January is the carnation. Legend says that Jesus' mother Mary shed tears as she watched Jesus carrying the cross upon which he died. Legend further says that when her tears fell to the ground, they became carnations. Carnations thus became a symbol of mother's love.

When the second Sunday in May was selected as a day to celebrate and honor motherhood in the United States, Ann Jaris, the leader of the "Mother's Day Movement," chose the carnation as a symbol of a mother's love. A colored carnation is worn if that person's mother is alive. A white carnation is worn if the person's mother has died.

January

As for the meaning behind the word, some scholars believe that the word carnation comes either from the word *coronation* (to crown the king) or *corone*, which were flower garlands used as Greek ceremonial crowns. The flowers in those crowns traditionally included carnations. Either base word reminds us of King Jesus.

Other scholars believe the word carnation originated from the Greek word *carnis* (meaning flesh), referring to the original color of the flower. *Carnis* can thus remind us of the incarnation of God made flesh—Jesus.

Unlike more delicate flowers, the carnation is strong and sturdy—staying fresh for many days. Also, unlike the sweeter fragrance of others flowers, the carnation is spicy. That spiciness can remind us of the spices—frankincense and myrrh—brought by the Wise Men as a gift to Jesus. On Epiphany.

The red carnation is the state flower of Ohio.

Garnets

The birthstone for the month of January is the garnet. The term "garnet" refers to a family of minerals. The garnet family contains gemstones in every color except blue, depending on what extra minerals they contain. For example, within the mineral family of "garnet" are tsavorites (green), hessonite (orange, brown and pink), and rhodolite (purplish red).

January

When we picture a garnet, however, most of us think of the deep blood red stone. Blood red. The color of Jesus' blood. A forever reminder of His sacrifice for us.

In gemstone symbolism, the garnet signifies eternal friendship and trust. Such as is found in Jesus, our eternal friend in whom we can place our trust.

In addition to crystal-like garnets, there are also star garnets. These garnets appear as pebble-like stones. The "star" (geologically referred to as "asterism") is produced by a sphere of tiny rods composed of titanium dioxide. These rods reflect light back out of the garnet and appear to our eye as a 4 or 6-rayed star that moves across the face of the gemstone as the stone is rotated. Star garnets are only found in India and Idaho. With the combination of Christmas and the Wise Men's arrival in Bethlehem, a star is an easy reminder of Jesus.

The garnet is known for its luminosity and high refractive quality. Because of those qualities, early travelers carried garnets, which they believed lit up the night and protected a person from evil. Some biblical scholars suggest that Noah used a lantern made from garnet to help him see through the storms while on the ark. Evidently, the garnet reminded Noah of Jesus, too.

The star garnet is the state gemstone of Idaho; the grossular garnet is the state gemstone of Vermont; the almandine garnet is the state gemstone of New York.

January

Need a Birthday Cake?

Many cultures begin the New Year with a "king cake" to celebrate the Wise Men's visit with Jesus. The cake would traditionally be baked on Twelfth Night (the twelfth day after Christmas Eve—yes those Twelve Days of Christmas), with Epiphany falling on the day after Twelfth Night. People would traditionally bake a coin or tiny plastic baby into the cake to represent Jesus. The person who received the piece of cake with the item was supposed to have extra good luck that year. Or they would undertake special obligations required of them.

King cakes from France (*gallette des rois*) are generally layers of puff pastry filled with almond cream. King cakes from Spain (*rosca de reyes*) are generally yeast bread decorated with candied fruit. King cakes from New Orleans (eaten also during *Mardi Gras*) are usually yeast bread, often filled with cream cheese or fruit. In Greece, the *vasilopita*, is either a dough bread or sweet cake, eaten any time between the New Year and Epiphany.

Since different cultures make this cake differently, we can celebrate the month of January with any cake we like. Here's an easy, Americanized version of a king cake, incorporating the fun of finding a coin inside and the deliciousness of...cake.

To honor the spicy fragrance of the carnation, the base of this cake is a boxed spice cake. Add apples, often used in the French *gallette des rois* and the Louisiana king cake.

For a traditional Louisiana king cake, make sure the frosting colors are *mardi gras* colors: purple, green and yellow. Purple represents justice, green represents faith and yellow represents power—all of which remind us of Jesus.

King Jesus Cake

1 boxed spice cake mix
2 eggs
1 cup milk
½ cup water
½ cup oil
1 can apple pie filling

Mix all thoroughly, then stir in the washed coin or plastic baby. Pour into greased sheet cake pan. Bake 350 degrees for 30-35 minutes or until toothpick comes out clean. Cool.

Cream Cheese Icing

¾ cup shortening
1 tsp clear vanilla
½ cup milk
8 ounces cream cheese
2-1/2 pound powdered sugar

Beat shortening, cream cheese and flavor. Add milk and sugar. Beat well.

Divide icing into thirds. Stir in purple food coloring into one third; green food coloring into a second third and yellow food

January

coloring into the third. Spread on cake, in stripes or blob it onto the cooled cake and swirl.

If you don't have purple food coloring, you can mix red and blue although it sometimes turns a gray-ish purple. Actual purple food coloring works best. Have fun!

Sharing Jesus with Others

Who do you know who has a birthday in January?

What about the month of January, the carnation or garnets would be of interest to that person?

How can you use that information to introduce them to Jesus?

What can you pray about for this person right now?

PRAYER: Heavenly Father, thank you for all the people born in January and for the lives lived for you. Thank you especially for Jesus. Show us things in this world daily that will remind us of you, Jesus. Then help us find ways to share you with others. Amen.

February: Irises, Violets, Amethyst & Valentines

You have made my days a mere handbreadth; the span of my years is as nothing before you. Everyone is but a breath, even those who seem secure (Psalm 39:5-6).

Let's Talk about February

February was named after *februa*, the Roman festival of purification which occurred during that month. Because Jesus died for our sins, we no longer need to undergo spiritual purification by human hands, in the form of animal sacrifices. Jesus did that for us, by providing a sacrifice that purified us from our sins—eternally.

The Roman purification process usually involved washing with water. Jesus referred to Himself as the living water, providing a way not only to wash us clean spiritually but to satisfy our spiritual thirst as well.

February

February holds a holiday that should always remind us of Jesus—Valentine's Day. We usually picture cupids and doilies, roses and hearts. But Valentine's Day is really all about love for Jesus.

Valentine's Day relates to early Christianity. Take another look at your calendar. Does it simply say Valentine's Day? Many calendars say St. Valentine's Day—because St. Valentine was a real-live person who lived a life for Christ. According to the Roman Catholic Church, Valentine was a Roman Catholic priest—a Christian martyr who died for his faith.

In 496 AD Pope Gelasius set February 14 as the date to celebrate St. Valentine's martyrdom. St. Valentine was known to have assisted Christians in the name of his love for Jesus, giving rise to our practice of focusing on love each February 14.

Now stores sell lacy cards, pink streamers and heart-shaped candies. Florists double the price of flowers and wives fix special dinners for husbands with candles lit and children sent to bed early. Lovers everywhere use the day as an excuse to broadcast their affection to the world. But the day originally was set aside as a holy day of God's church.

Getting past the greeting cards that display naked babies with wings, trays filled with chocolate dipped strawberries and tiny hearts munched by the mouthful, St. Valentine's Day reminds us of Jesus—the true author and giver of love. In fact, for those who know Jesus, every day is St. Valentine's Day.

Do everything in love (1 Corinthians 16:14).

February

Irises and Violets

The iris is the main flower for February. Its stalks are tall and sturdy; its flowers large and showy. Although we generally think of irises as purple, they come in all colors. In fact, the name "iris" comes from the Latin word for rainbow.

God's promise to mankind is represented visually in the sky every time we see a rainbow. The rainbow reminds us—and Him—of His everlasting love for us, ultimately made flesh through Jesus.

The leaves of the iris remind us of Jesus, too. They are sword shaped. The sword of God—according to Ephesians 6—is the Word of God. The Word of God, explained in John 1:14 is Jesus himself.

> *The Word became flesh and made his dwelling among us. We have seen his glory, the glory of the one and only Son, who came from the Father, full of grace and truth* (John 1:14).

The word "iris" also refers to the part of our eye that helps focus our vision. It is the eyeball muscle, the thing that expands and contracts to control the size of our pupil. Jesus recognized the relationship between seeing physically and seeing spiritually, when He asked the disciples:

> *"Do you have eyes but fail to see, and ears but fail to hear?"* (Mark 8:17-18)

February

The iris flower then can be a reminder to see through Jesus' eyes. To look where He points. To focus on Him.

The violet is the secondary flower for February. The small, soft blossoms and velvety leaves remind us that humility, humbleness and gentleness are precious to God. Its name reflects the color most common to violets—purple, the color of royalty. The color of King Jesus.

Both the iris and the violet represent faith and hope. More than anything, this reminds us that the basis for our hope of heaven is our faith in Jesus.

The Iris is the state flower of Tennessee. The violet is the state flower of Illinois, New Jersey, Rhode Island and Wisconsin.

Amethyst

The birthstone for the month of February is the amethyst. Amethyst is just quartz. Quartz is the second most abundant mineral in the Earth's crust, after feldspar. But as quartz goes, purple amethyst is the most precious of the varieties of quartz. And perhaps the loveliest.

In gemstone symbolism, amethyst symbolizes heavenly understanding, spiritual contentment and the unity between mind, body and spirit. Can you say Holy Spirit? God, through the Holy Spirit, lives in us—our bodies, His temple.

February

According to the Book of Revelation 21:20, one of the 12 foundations of heaven is amethyst—giving us a glimpse that heaven, founded on lovely amethyst—will be amazing in its heavenly beauty!

Amethyst is the state gemstone of South Carolina.

The Color Purple

Both birth flowers and the birthstone for February are purple. The color purple also reminds us of Jesus.

Lydia, one of the New Testament women mentioned in Acts 16:14 had a business selling purple cloth to rich people. Most people couldn't afford to wear purple, because the die was made from one specific type of clam, found in the Middle East. The die was a costly process to create.

Purple cloth eventually became so expensive that in medieval times, no one but royalty wore purple. To this day, purple is considered to be the color of nobility. Jesus, the King of Kings, is most worthy of all to wear the purple color of royalty.

And in fact, He did.

> *Then Pilate took Jesus and had him flogged. The soldiers twisted together a crown of thorns and put it on his head. They clothed him in a purple robe and went up to him again and again,*

saying, "Hail, king of the Jews!" And they struck him in the face. (John 19:1-3)

Purple is a combination of the colors red and blue. In color symbolism, red is associated with war, blood and judgment. Blue is associated with law and commandment. Jesus—as God incarnate—represents both judgment and the commandments, made new and made possible through his blood sacrifice. In other words, purple is the color of Jesus.

Need a Birthday Cake?

February 3 is National Carrot Cake Day so February is a great month to share this recipe. For extra fun, use heart-shaped cake pans and celebrate National Carrot Cake Day and St. Valentine's Day together.

I Love Carrot Cake

1-1/2 cup oil
2 cup sugar
3 cups finely grated carrots
1 tsp cinnamon
½ tsp salt
4 eggs
1 cup chopped walnuts or pecans
2 cups flour
2 tsp baking soda.

February

Beat eggs, oil and sugar. Add dry ingredients. Mix in carrots and nuts. Pour into 2 greased and floured 8 or 9" cake pans. Bake at 350 for 35-40 minutes. Cool and frost.

Cream Cheese Frosting

Cream together:

½ cup softened butter
8 ounces softened cream cheese
1tsp vanilla
1 box powdered sugar

Sharing Jesus with Others

Who do you know who has a birthday in February?

What about the month of February, irises, violets, amethyst or the color purple would be of interest to that person?

How can you use that information to introduce them to Jesus?

What can you pray about for this person right now?

February

PRAYER: Heavenly Father, thank you for the people born in February. Jesus, as the King of Glory, you have the ultimate right to wear the purple robes of majesty. Please remind us that in your creation of the beautiful iris, violet and amethyst, you have hidden a tiny glimpse of the glory waiting for us with you in heaven. Help us share that beauty with others. Amen.

March: Daffodils, Aquamarine & Lent

"In the time of my favor I heard you, and in the day of salvation I helped you." I tell you, now is the time of God's favor, now is the day of salvation (2 Corinthians 6:1-2).

Let's Talk about March

Although Easter is tied in with the Jewish calendar and is therefore not on the same date each year, we generally think of April as Easter month. Therefore, Lent, the 6 weeks leading up to Easter, occurs partly during the month of March—sometimes beginning in February; sometimes extending into April.

The name of the month of March comes from reference to the Roman *Martius* and honors the Roman god, Mars. In mythology, Mars was the Roman god who controlled war.

March

Although we know Jesus as the epitome of love, Scripture also tells us that there is a spiritual battle going on between God and Satan. In fact, Scripture reminds us that a spiritual battle surrounds us with Jesus fighting against Satan for our very soul.

> *Finally, be strong in the Lord and in his mighty power. Put on the full armor of God, so that you can take your stand against the devil's schemes. For our struggle is not against flesh and blood, but against the rulers, against the authorities, against the powers of this dark world and against the spiritual forces of evil in the heavenly realms. Therefore put on the full armor of God, so that when the day of evil comes, you may be able to stand your ground, and after you have done everything, to stand* (Ephesians 6:10-13).

Thus, although Jesus preached His love for us and our need to love others in His name, the Apostle John's visions in the Book of Revelation remind us that Jesus is the true God of war.

> *I saw heaven standing open and there before me was a white horse, whose rider is called Faithful and True. With justice he judges and wages war. His eyes are like blazing fire, and on his head are many crowns. He has a name written on him that no one knows but he himself. He is*

March

dressed in a robe dipped in blood, and his name is the Word of God. The armies of heaven were following him, riding on white horses and dressed in fine linen, white and clean. Coming out of his mouth is a sharp sword with which to strike down the nations. (Revelation 19:11-15).

The month of March may have originally been named for the Roman god of war, but fortunately Jesus is in charge and the battle belongs to Him. We win.

Daffodils

The delightful daffodil grows from a bulb. When the blossoms above ground die, the bulb below goes dormant throughout the fall and winter, returning to blossom again in the springtime. It is one of the first flowers to bloom in spring, signaling the end of the dead season. It is therefore a classic symbol of rebirth, the resurrection of Jesus and our being born again in Him.

The daffodil is also a traditional symbol of friendship, reminding us of the song: *What a friend we have in Jesus*. It also reminds us of one of the last things Jesus said before returning to heaven: that He was leaving the Holy Spirit to be our guide, our counselor and our friend.

The daffodil is also a symbol of domestic happiness. Philippians 3:20 says that our citizenship is in heaven. Earth is our temporary home. Our true and eternal home is heaven. And when we get there, we'll have true domestic happiness. It makes us wonder if heaven will be filled with daffodils.

Aquamarine

The birthstone for the month of March is aquamarine. The word aquamarine means "water of the sea." Genesis tells us that in the beginning, the Spirit of God hovered over the water. Later, Jesus became the living water. Water itself—in the Christian practice of symbolically proclaiming our faith through baptism by water—points us toward Jesus. All of us need water to live here on earth. We need the living water for eternal life in heaven.

The aquamarine gemstone is believed to enhance divine communication and help us connect with heaven. Spiritual metaphysics notwithstanding, gazing at the cool, clear blue of aquamarine gives a person a sense of well-being. Spending time with God does so even better.

Aquamarine is the state gemstone of Colorado.

March

Need a Birthday Cake?

How about a "war cake" in honor of the Roman god Mars? Or better yet, in honor of Jesus?

During World War II it was common to create new recipes to make a tasty treat without using up all of the family's sugar rations. Evidently my family modified their recipe after the war because it's chock full of sugar. It's also completely yummy!

Jesus' War Cake

Stew a box of raisins in 2 cups of water in a slow boil until water is ½ gone. Remove from stove and add:

1 cup cold water
½ cup shortening
2 cups sugar
1 tsp ground cloves
1 tsp cinnamon
1 Tablespoon baking soda
4 cups flour
1 tsp salt
1 tsp nutmeg

Mix together. Bake at 375 degrees for 45 minutes in an angel food or Bundt cake pan. Cool for 10 minutes and then turn out onto a platter.

March

Buttermilk Icing

2 cups sugar
½ cup brown sugar
½ cup margarine or butter
1 cup buttermilk
½ tsp baking soda
1 Tablespoon vanilla
2 Tablespoons light Karo syrup

Stir together in medium sauce pan and bring to boil. Lower heat and boil on low until it reaches "soft ball stage" (drop small amount from a spoon into very cold water. It should become a soft ball when squeezed between your fingers).

Cool for about 10 minutes and then pour over cake. Eat cake warm or cool.

Sharing Jesus with Others

Who do you know who has a birthday in March?

What about the month of March, the daffodil or aquamarine would be of interest to that person?

How can you use that information to introduce them to Jesus?

What can you pray about for this person right now?

March

PRAYER: Heavenly Father, thank you all the people born in March. Thank you also for the beauty of springtime and the reminders of rebirth and of our eternal home in heaven. Help us to see you in everything around us. Help us to look for you and to be reminded of your character. And then to praise you for it. Amen.

April: Sweet Peas, Daisies, Diamonds & Easter

My times are in your hands (Psalm 31:15).

Let's Talk About April

In the Roman calendar, April was the month set aside for Venus, the Roman goddess of love. Some scholars suggest that the name of the month, April—from the Roman name for the month, *Aprilis*—was originally *Aphrilis* taken from the Greek goddess' name Aphrodite, which was the equivalent to Venus in the Roman/Greek list of gods and goddesses.

Our God, however, is and forever shall be the true God of love.

April

For God so loved the world that he gave his one and only Son, that whoever believes in him shall not perish but have eternal life (John 3:16).

God, the Father proved His love for us by sending His son, Jesus. Jesus, God the Son, proved His love for us by dying for our sins. God, the Holy Spirit proved His love for us by living in us, being our guide, our counselor and our friend. It all culminated on Easter Sunday.

Although Easter Sunday moves between the months of March and April, it is most often celebrated in April. When we think of Easter, we most often think of April.

Sweet Peas and Daisies

The sweet pea is fragrant, colorful and lacy as it dances in the spring breeze. And because it symbolizes happiness, it reminds us of Jesus, who is the source of our true joy.

April's second flower is the daisy. The daisy symbolizes innocence and certainty. No matter our past. No matter our sins. No matter our struggles; when we repent and receive Jesus, we are purified. His forgiveness washes us clean; purifies our soul. We are born again; innocent in his eyes. Of that we can be certain.

I like to imagine sitting with others at Jesus' feet as he holds an enormous bouquet of daisies. He would pick each petal and drop it softly on our heads, repeating, "I love you. I love you. I love you."

Because he does not know how to say, "I love you not."

The Black Eyed Susan, also called the Gloriosa Daisy, is the state flower of Maryland.

Diamonds

Have you ever seen a diamond in the rough? It's not so thrilling. It resembles simple quartz—often dull and full of spots. Sort of like us, before Jesus takes hold of our hearts and cleans us up from the inside out.

The diamond represents faithfulness, love, and purity, which is why the stone is traditionally used in engagement and wedding rings. But in gemstone symbolism, the diamond also symbolizes eternity. As does Jesus.

When shopping for diamonds, buyers are instructed to always look for the "four Cs." Those are color, clarity, carat, and cut. By focusing on the four Cs, a buyer can be assured of getting the best quality in this precious stone.

But as Christians, we too have the 4 Cs. They are the cross, Calvary, covenant, and commandments. And they are more precious than the most precious diamond.

The diamond is the state gemstone of Arkansas.

April

Need a Birthday Cake?

It's time for chocolate. In fact, it's time for a chocolate, chocolate, chocolate, chocolate, chocolate chip cake. Ready?

Five Times Chocolate Cake

1 fudge cake mix
1 small package chocolate pudding
1 cup sour cream
½ cup oil
4 eggs
½ cup water
1-1/2 cup chocolate chips

Mix together and pour into 2 greased and floured 8 or 9" cake pans. Bake at 350 for 40-45 minutes. Cool.

Spread with your favorite chocolate frosting on all sides and between. Sprinkle chocolate sprinkles on top. That's five forms of chocolate all in one cake. Yum!

Or, bake the cake in a Bundt cake pan. Invert the cake while still warm, but not hot, onto a serving platter. When cool, sprinkle with powdered sugar. Just remember what happens to powdered sugar when blowing out the candles. It's like a snow shower in springtime.

April

Sharing Jesus with Others

Who do you know who has a birthday in April?

What about the month of April, sweet peas, daisies or diamonds would be of interest to that person?

How can you use that information to introduce them to Jesus?

What can you pray about for this person right now?

PRAYER: Heavenly Father, thank you for the people born in April. Thank you also for the reminders in nature of your character and your love for us. Thank you that every petal on every flower tells us of your love. Amen.

May: Lilies of the Valley, Emeralds & Mom

> *With all wisdom and understanding, he made known to us the mystery of his will according to his good pleasure, which he purposed in Christ, to be put into effect when the times reach their fulfillment—to bring unity to all things in heaven and on earth under Christ* (Ephesians 1:8-10).

Let's Talk About May

In Roman mythology, *Maia* (meaning "the great one") was the goddess of spring.

> *See! The winter is past; the rains are over and gone. Flowers appear on the earth; the season of singing has come, the cooing of doves is heard in our land* (Song of Solomon 2:11-12).

Our God is the creator and lover of variety. In His wisdom, God made seasons, allowing variety even in weather patterns and temperatures. With springtime beginning at the end of March,

May

by the time May has arrived, we have enjoyed the spring season and are now looking forward to the next variety of season in June when summer arrives.

May is also the month we celebrate Mother's Day. Motherhood requires patience, guidance and the placing of the interests of others above her own. Jesus teaches us to pursue the same things in our lives.

Mother's Day also reminds us that when Jesus set aside His heavenly residence to live among us, He had an earthly mother. And—wise mother that Mary was—her words (to a servant at the wedding of Canaan) record an eternal truth for us to follow in all circumstances:

> "Do whatever [Jesus] tells you" (John 2:5, explanation added).

Lilies of the Valley

The flower for the month of May is the lily of the valley. Lilies of the valley are tiny and delicate and often grow wild. They remind us of what Jesus said:

> *"Consider how the lilies grow. They do not labor or spin. Yet I tell you, not even Solomon in all his splendor was dressed like one of these"* (Luke 12:27).

May

It's just like Jesus to focus on the small things we might otherwise not pay attention to—such as mustard seeds, children, sparrows, tiny lilies. When looked at up close, the beauty of the lily of the valley is undeniable, with little bells that silently chime God's praise. They are dressed in splendor. By God.

Jesus is often referred to as the "Rose of Sharon," which references the Song of Songs 2:1:

> *I am a rose of Sharon, a lily of the valleys.*

Although the context of Song of Songs is Solomon's love for his wife, many biblical scholars believe the book represents Jesus' desire for a love relationship with us.

> *Even though I walk through the valley of the shadow of death, I will fear no evil, for you are with me* (Psalm 23:4).

When was the last time you walked through a shadowed valley of despair, sorrow or crisis? When we do, maybe those valleys are covered with lilies; filled with sweet-smelling reminders of God's love and presence. Maybe we just have to stop and see them.

Several Psalms begin with notations: to be sung to the tune of Lilies. (Psalm 45, Psalm 60; Psalm 69; Psalm 80) We don't know what the tune sounds like, but it must have been beautiful to God and to men for its reference to have been preserved in Scripture. So too should our lives be beautiful to

God; our songs to Him filled with praise and clothed in splendor.

The lily of the valley is described by botanists as a "hardy" plant, often grown amid thorns. Jesus was forced to wear a crown of thorns—taking us back again to Song of Songs 2:2 like a lily among thorns...

...and reminding us of Jesus.

Emeralds

The birthstone for the month of May is the emerald. It symbolizes rebirth, reminding us of Jesus' resurrection as well as our rebirth into God's family when we come to Christ.

Several healing properties have been mythically associated with the emerald. The one that makes me smile is that gazing upon an emerald supposedly soothes the eyes. Well, of course it does. It's just that beautiful. As is our Lord when we gaze upon Him.

Ancient Greeks and Romans, associated emeralds with Aphrodite/Venus—their goddess of love. Our God—the one true God of love—proved His love by the physical act of becoming human and dying for our sake. In Christian symbolism then, the emerald stands for rebirth in Christ, faith and hope and love.

May

So faith, hope, love abide, these three; but the greatest of these is love (1 Corinthians 13:13).

Sort of makes you want to go find an emerald and gaze upon its beauty, doesn't it?

The emerald is the state gemstone of North Carolina.

Need a Birthday Cake?

Pineapple upside down cakes are perfect for springtime. This is a twist on a traditional upside down cake. It's made in two layers, which makes it extra moist. Also, using crushed pineapple instead of rings makes the cake easy to slice—handy when you go for second helpings!

Pineapple Inside Out Cake

1 packaged yellow cake mix
Oil and eggs according to the box directions

Substitute the drained pineapple juice for the amount of water needed.

Melt ½ cup butter or margarine and pour equal amounts into two 8 or 9-inch round cake pans. Sprinkle ½ cup brown sugar into each pan, covering butter. Spread ½ of the crushed pineapple evenly between the two pans.

Pour batter evenly between the two pans and bake according to directions. You may need to allow additional time because of the fruit.

Let cakes cool completely. Then turn one of the cakes upside down onto a cake plate. Then turn the second cake upside down onto the first. Yes, really. No frosting needed between them.

The cake can be eaten immediately but it's even better the next day when the juices have seeped more deeply into the cake.

Of course, you can also just make this a one-layer cake, but it's even more fun with two layers—you could almost call it an upside down, inside out cake.

Sharing Jesus with Others

Who do you know who has a birthday in May?

What about the month of May, lilies of the valley or emeralds would be of interest to that person?

How can you use that information to introduce them to Jesus?

What can you pray about for this person right now?

May

PRAYER: Heavenly Father, thank you for the people born in May. Thank you also for giving splendor to even the smallest things you have created to provide us with an opportunity to exclaim your glory. Amen.

June: Roses, Pearls & the Gospel

∼

(Make) the most of every opportunity, because the days are evil (Ephesians 5:16).

Let's Talk About June

June was named in the Roman calendar after Juno, the principle goddess of the Romans. She was Jupiter's wife and thus was the goddess of marriage and the well-being of women. Since June was named for the goddess of marriage, is it any wonder that June is one of the most popular months for weddings?

Then again, every month is a time to think about weddings, because Jesus has told us that we—who make up His church—are being prepared as His holy bride.

June

Let us rejoice and be glad and give him glory! For the wedding of the Lamb has come, and his bride has made herself ready (Revelation 19:7).

No, this won't be a wedding like we have on earth. It will be even better. We are preparing ourselves now, growing our relationship with Jesus and being faithful to Him. One day, He will take us home and we will live with Him forever.

Roses

The Rose is the flower for the month of June. Roses are simply in a class by themselves—elegant and graceful. Neither can the beauty that was Jesus' life be compared to any other human who ever lived or who will ever live. Jesus is beautiful beyond compare.

The rose is also strong and tall. It does not trail like a sweet pea. It does not bend like a tulip. It is not short like a violet or fragile like lilies of the valley. The rose blossom stands on a strong stem, nearly wood-like in its strength. Its bush can even be trained to grow as a tree. We gain strength through Jesus; we can rely on His strength when we have none of our own. We can stand tall for Him.

The rose has thorns. Symbolic thorns are part of our lives. Thorns are part of who we are—those character flaws that God is working on; those "thorns in our sides" that Paul referred to. Although perfect and without symbolic thorns, Jesus wore real thorns, shaped into a crown by His persecutors as He carried His cross and our sins to Calvary. The rose reminds us of our thorns and that Christ died for them, by taking them on Himself.

Roses are a beautiful reflection of God's beauty. But He gave them a short life. Two weeks if you take special care of cut roses. Jesus' life was short in human terms. But what He accomplished was powerful and eternal. Doesn't God want us to live our short lives in a powerful way, too? In a way that will have eternal consequences?

Roses reflect God's desire for us: to live with recognition of His beauty; with grace for others; and with strength in our faith as He works to remove our thorns. He wants us to live our short lives in a glorious manner. For Him.

Varieties of the rose are the state flower of Georgia, Iowa, New York, North Dakota and Oklahoma.

Pearls

June is the one month of the year whose birth "stone"—the pearl—isn't a stone at all. The pearl is actually created inside an oyster when a bit of irritant, such as a grain of sand or parasite, gets inside the shell. The oyster then secretes the same mineral that lines its shell—calcium carbonate—to coat the irritant and protect the oyster. Over time, the layers of calcium carbonate build up to create a pearl.

Throughout history, society has considered pearls to be rare, beautiful and valuable. In Scripture, pearls are symbols of the Gospel.

> *"Again, the kingdom of heaven is like a merchant looking for fine pearls. When he found one of great value, he went away and sold everything he had and bought it"* (Matthew 13:45-46).

Jesus' parable reminds us that our salvation through Him, is priceless. Deepening our faith and relationship with Him, should be our number one priority.

Pearls also remind us of Jesus because of how they're made. Pearls are the oyster's way of protecting itself from a harsh irritant. Jesus protects us from painful things in life—if we but lean on Him. In fact, just like an oyster, God can create layers of soothing protection from the irritants of life. Those layers become our ever-deeper faith; a faith that is beautiful, rare and valuable.

So valuable that we should do everything we can to make it our own; because it results in our being part of God's kingdom of heaven.

And we know what the pearly gates of heaven are made of.

June

The twelve gates were twelve pearls, each gate made of a single pearl. The great street of the city was of gold, as pure as transparent glass (Revelation 21:21).

June's birthstone can't be found in any underground mine on earth. Pearls are created by living creatures; much like the foundation of our faith is based on trust in a living God.

Pearls require no faceting or polishing to reveal their natural beauty. Just like our faith in Jesus requires nothing but to believe—and then trust and obey. That's a beautiful thing.

Freshwater pearls are the state gemstone of Kentucky and Tennessee.

Need a Birthday Cake?

A cheesecake isn't really a cake; it's almost more like a pie. But then a pearl isn't really a stone. So maybe cheesecake isn't a traditional birthday cake. But it could be.

This recipe is easy to use and comes out lovely every time. Top with fresh fruit, your favorite canned variety or nothing at all.

June

Smile and Say Cheese-Cake

2 8-ounce packages cream cheese (softened)
½ tsp vanilla
½ cup sugar
2 eggs

Graham Cracker Crust

1-1/2 cups fine graham cracker crumbs
1/3 cup sugar
6 Tablespoons melted butter

Mix until well blended. Press into pan.

Spread cracker mixture into bottom of spring form cake pan. Mix other ingredients and pour into crust. Bake at 350 for 40 minutes.

Cool and then refrigerate for at least three hours. Top with fruit or eat plain.

June

Sharing Jesus with Others

Who do you know who has a birthday in June?

What about the month of June, roses or pearls would be of interest to that person?

How can you use that information to introduce them to Jesus?

What can you pray about for this person right now?

PRAYER: Heavenly Father, thank you for the people born in June. Thank you also for showing us your truth in the parables you spoke so long ago. Please remind us each day of the Gospel's incomparable value and help us find new ways to make it a deeper part of our lives and to share it with others. Amen.

July: Larkspurs, Lilies, Rubies & Freedom

But since we belong to the day, let us be sober, putting on faith and love as a breastplate, and the hope of salvation as a helmet. For God did not appoint us to suffer wrath but to receive salvation through our Lord Jesus Christ. He died for us so that, whether we are awake or asleep, we may live together with him. Therefore encourage one another and build each other up, just as in fact you are doing (1 Thessalonians 5:8-11).

Let's Talk About July

When Julius Caesar reformed the Roman calendar he added two months to the old 10-month calendar. He then named one of the two months after himself—Julius—which we have shortened to July.

July

The biggest holiday we celebrate during July in America is Independence Day. The focus is freedom and it is joyous. We are ever thankful to those who died to give us the political freedom we have in this country.

But Jesus also died for our freedom—our freedom from the condemnation and eternal judgment of our sins.

> *Now the Lord is the Spirit, and where the Spirit of the Lord is, there is freedom* (2 Corinthians 3:17).

More precisely, our freedom is in Christ:

> *Then you will know the truth, and the truth will set you free* (John 8:32).

Because what is truth?

> *Jesus answered, "I am the way and the truth and the life"* (John 14:6).

We have freedom because we have truth—Jesus. Every day is therefore a day to celebrate our freedom because of what Jesus has done for us.

July

Larkspurs and Lilies

The Larkspur is a glorious, stalked flower lined with brilliant blossoms in white, pink, blue, or violet. The shape of each blossom is a 5-pointed star. The star shape reminds us of the star that pointed the way to Bethlehem for the Wise Men and the shepherds. The star symbol can still point us to Jesus.

The bird, the lark, in literature is often portrayed as singing hymns and prayers at the gate of heaven. And as it announces the new day, the lark symbolizes hope made new. While most birds can only sing while perched, a lark can also sing while flying. This ability reminds us to find joy in everything we do and that we find our true joy and hope in Jesus.

In Near Eastern mythology, the lark is associated with the spirit of wheat. In real life, the lark helps rid wheat fields of destructive pests. The lark has become a symbol for Christ who is "the living bread which came down from heaven" (John 6:51). It is through Jesus that our destructive sins are forgiven.

In Genesis 3:15 God told Adam and Eve:

> *"I will put enmity between you and the woman, and between your offspring and hers; he will crush your head, and you will strike his heel."*

The larkspur is sometimes called the lark's claw or lark's heel. With very little imagination, we can see this as a subtle reference to Jesus' heel and as he crushed Satan.

July

The water lily is the second flower for July. Who but God would have created a flower that grows in water? There are cactus flowers that grow in sand. There are egret flowers that grow in bogs. There are flowers that grow in rock crevices, mulch, fungus and rich soil. But water? Only the God of the universe could think of that—and then call Himself the "living water."

The water lily is also known as the lotus. It is symbolic in many cultures of sacred enlightenment. Think meditation and the practice in yoga of meditating on a lotus blossoming open. Now think Jesus. Our true sacred enlightenment.

To the ancient Egyptians, the lotus symbolized the sun and rebirth. Jesus is not the sun; but the Son. And He came to make us born again and to assure us that we will live with Him in eternity.

Buddhists consider the water lily a symbol of purity and divine birth. Hello, Jesus.

Rubies

The birthstone for July is the ruby. In gemstone symbolism, the ruby's dark red color represents Jesus' blood sacrifice for us. That sacrifice is everlasting—one sacrifice for all people for all time.

July

The ruby is a variety of the corundum gem family; a lasting gemstone, durable enough to wear every day. Just like the ruby, Jesus' salvation is durable enough for us to "put on" and wear every day—as the armor of God (Ephesians 6:10-18).

John's vision of Heaven reveals the appearance of God:

> *And the one who sat there* [on the throne] *had the appearance of jasper and ruby* (Revelation 4:3, explanation added).

Interestingly, both the jasper and ruby are typically red in color. Also interestingly, jasper is partially stone and partly organic—just like God in the person of Jesus, is both wholly God and wholly organic man. But that tidbit is for another discussion... Of relevance here is that in the Book of Revelation God describes His own appearance as similar to July's birthstone.

Scripture also compares wisdom to rubies.

> *...for wisdom is more precious than rubies, and nothing you desire can compare with her* (Proverbs 8:11).

> *...the price of wisdom is beyond rubies* (Job 28:18).

God wants us to be wise. And He recognizes that wisdom is precious. So then, we too, should strive to achieve wisdom in all things. The best wisdom comes from God—as we seek His desires through Scripture, meditation and prayer.

In fact, the helmet of salvation that is part of our armor of God protects our thinking and thus can grant godly wisdom. I wouldn't be surprised if our heavenly helmets are studded with rubies.

For the gals in the crowd, Proverbs 31:10 is a great reminder:

> *A wife of noble character who can find? She is worth far more than rubies.*

Speaking from the female perspective, a husband of noble character is worth far more than rubies, too. In fact, shouldn't we all strive to live like rubies for Jesus?

Need a Birthday Cake?

To celebrate the freedom we have because of Jesus (and the fourth of July), here's a fun red-white-and blue cake that has been popular since the 1950s. Change the colors and flavors throughout the year to suit the holiday or birthday person's preference.

July

Freedom Cake

Make a standard white cake, using your favorite mix. Cook it in two round cake pans.

After the cake has cooled for 15 minutes, poke holes in the cake top with a fork, allowing the fork to go into the cake about 2 inches.

Dissolve one package of red gelatin in 1 cup of boiling water. Cool it slightly and then pour it over one of the cooling cakes, using enough to cover it well. You may have some remaining.

Dissolve one package of blue gelatin in 1 cup of boiling water, cool slightly and pour it over the second cake. Chill completely.

Remove one cake onto a cake plate. Top with whipping cream. Unmold the second cake and place it on top of the first. Frost the top and sides with whipping cream.

Add an equal amount of cold water to the amount of each gelatin remaining, chill and eat separately if you wish.

You might use red and green gelatin for a lively Christmas cake later in the year. Lemon gelatin is good any time.

July

Sharing Jesus with Others

Who do you know who has a birthday in July?

What about the month of July, larkspurs, lilies, rubies or garnets would be of interest to that person?

How can you use that information to introduce them to Jesus?

What can you pray about for this person right now?

PRAYER: Heavenly Father, thank you for the people born in July. Thank you also for the variety and beauty you created when you created this world. Open our eyes and help us see more of your glory. And please remind us of the freedom we have because of you. Amen.

August: Gladiolus, Poppies, Peridot & Priests

~

Now listen, you who say, "Today or tomorrow we will go to this or that city, spend a year there, carry on business and make money." Why, you do not even know what will happen tomorrow. What is your life? You are a mist that appears for a little while and then vanishes. Instead, you ought to say, "If it is the Lord's will, we will live and do this or that" (James 4:13-15).

Let's Talk About August

Augustus Caesar clarified and completed the calendar reform began by Julius Caesar. When two months were added to the former 10-month calendar, one was named after Julius Caesar (July) and one after Augustus Caesar (August.)

August

August is a bit slow in the holiday department. But there are still oodles of "national days"—holidays made up for the fun of it. One of the best is "National Friendship Day" which occurs on the first Sunday in August.

Scripture reminds us that we are to treat others as we would have them treat us. We are to love our enemies. We are to consider others better than ourselves.

> *I no longer call you servants, because a servant does not know his master's business. Instead, I have called you friends, for everything that I learned from my Father I have made known to you* (John 15:15).

Jesus calls us friends. Wow.

Scripture also reminds us that Jesus left us the Holy Spirit—as our guide, counselor and friend. That is cause to celebrate every day, but at least once a year.

Coincidently, Friendship Day, the first Sunday of August, is also International Forgiveness Day. It's probably not a coincidence, after all.

August

Gladiolus and Poppies

The gladiolus stands tall and straight, its blossoms in a row, announcing to all the world its symbolism of strength and sincerity. The gladiolus is often the frame upon which the florist creates. The backdrop for the arrangement. The strength for the display of color and beauty.

Many people assume that the root meaning of the word gladiolus is that they are flowers that make you glad. In reality, the gladiolus was named after the gladiator. Its Latin root, *gladius* literally means sword. The flower is even sometimes called the "sword lily." The gladiolus is a warrior's flower.

We are called to be in Jesus' army and to fight evil around us. To do so, Ephesians 6:11-17 reminds us to put on the full armor of God. One part of that armor is the sword of the Spirit; which is the word of God. The gladiolus, the "sword lily," reflects both the power and the beauty of Scripture.

In Roman times, gladiators who lost fights were cast into a pit. So too should we be on judgment day, sinful that we are. Fortunately, we have Jesus. Jesus died so we wouldn't be cast into the pit. He will fight with and for us. Every day.

The poppy is the second flower of August. It grows in fields, spreading out as far as the eye can see. Low to the ground, waving in the breeze. Fluid, gentle, tender. The poppy is the state flower of California. Despite its exuberant growth in the

August

wild—covering meadows and poking out of beach grass—it is illegal to pick the flower in California. It is precious.

One of the best images of poppies is from the movie, *The Wizard of Oz*. Dorothy and her friends climb a hill and look out into the valley ahead. "Poppies!" they exclaim before bounding, leaping and skipping into their midst. Yes, the poppies were poisoned by the wicked witch, but their sight was joyful. And despite the poison, our stalwart friends didn't gasp and choke. They simply lay down in the midst of the pleasant meadow and drifted off to sleep. That image reminds us of Psalm 23:

> *Even though I walk through the darkest valley, I will fear no evil, for you are with me.*

I wonder. When we walk through the darkest valley, is it possible that the valley floor is actually covered with spiritual poppies, along with the lilies of the valley we learned about in May?

Has God provided a soft meadow for us to rest in during our journey through the dark valley? Will Jesus wake us gently, when we are renewed and ready to complete the journey?

The gladiolus is about strength, named for some of the fiercest warriors in history. The poppy is a gentle flower, growing wild and free. Taken together, perhaps we need both the strength of the warrior gladiolus and the gentleness of the poppy in our lives, both of which Jesus can provide. What an unusual and beautiful bouquet they make when placed together and tied with the ribbon of faith.

Peridot

The birthstone for the month of August is peridot. It is a biblical gemstone. Translations of mineral names from Hebrew, Greek, and Aramaic to English are not always exact. Most scholars and historians, however, believe that the green stone referred to in Bible translations as chrysolite, is beautiful lime-green peridot.

Ezekiel says peridot (chrysolite) was present in the Garden of Eden:

> *You were in Eden, the garden of God; every precious stone adorned you: carnelian,* **chrysolite** *and emerald, topaz, onyx and jasper, lapis lazuli, turquoise and beryl* (Ezekiel 28:13, emphasis added).

In the Middle Ages, peridot was believed to have the power to drive away evil. Peridot was also named as one of the stones adorning the breastplate of the High Priest (Exodus 28) and represented the Tribe of Zebulun (the sixth son of Jacob and Leah). When the Hebrews entered the Promised Land, the Tribe of Zebulun's inheritance was generally the territory toward the Sea of Galilee where Jesus conducted his Galilean ministry. Thus it also included Bethlehem—the birthplace of Jesus.

In ancient Jewish times, only the High Priest was allowed to wear the jeweled Breastplate. Because Jesus became our High Priest forever though, Jesus now symbolically wears the

Breastplate of the High Priest—and August's birthstone, the peridot—forever.

The Apostle John shares his vision of heaven, saying,

> *The foundations of the city walls were decorated with every kind of precious stone. The first foundation was jasper, the second sapphire, the third agate, the fourth emerald, the fifth onyx, the sixth ruby, the seventh chrysolite, the eighth beryl, the ninth topaz, the tenth turquoise, the eleventh jacinth, and the twelfth amethyst (Revelation 21:19).*

Did you see? The seventh layer (the number of perfection in biblical symbolism) of the foundation of heaven is peridot.

Need a Birthday Cake?

A lemon poppy seed cake is perfect for summer. It is light, refreshing and always delicious. And since the poppy is one of the flowers for the month of August, it is especially appropriate.

If you don't know anyone who has a birthday in August, you can always make this cake and invite someone over on the first Sunday of the month. Or make any day National Friendship Day!

August

Lemon Poppy Seed Cake

1 package yellow cake mix
1 cup water
½ cup oil
4 eggs
1 package instant lemon pudding
4 Tablespoons poppy seeds

Mix all and pour into greased and floured Bundt cake pan.

Bake at 350 for 45 minutes.

Icing: mix 2 cups powdered sugar and 3-4 tablespoons fresh lemon juice. Drizzle over the top of the cake.

Sharing Jesus with Others

Who do you know who has a birthday in August?

What about the month of August, the gladiolas, poppies or peridot would be of interest to that person?

How can you use that information to introduce them to Jesus?

What can you pray about for this person right now?

August

PRAYER: Heavenly Father, thank you for the people born in August. Please help us to live strong and joyful lives for you. Remind us to put on the full armor of God each day, including the Sword which is your word. Remind us to be both warriors for you but to also have a glad and sincere heart for your plan and how to treat others with gentleness. Amen.

September: Asters, Glories, Sapphires & Saviors

A thousand years in your sight are like a day that has just gone by, or like a watch in the night (Psalm 90:4).

Let's Talk About September

Sept is a Latin prefix meaning seven. When Caesar reformed the Roman calendar, two months were added to the previous ten. However, the order of the months were maintained. September had been the seventh month in the old Roman calendar—reflecting the meaning of the root prefix *sept*. Today, with our 12-month calendar, September is the ninth month. Who knows what Caesar was thinking in keeping the order the same?

The number seven or patterns of seven occur more than 700 times in Scripture. Seven is considered to be the perfect number and the number of completeness in numerology.

September

Seven is therefore often referred to as God's number. In Genesis—the very first book of the Bible, God created the universe in 6 days and then rested on the seventh. Creation was complete.

That doesn't necessarily mean the month of September is perfect. After all, Caesar's maintenance of September's name despite it being the ninth month makes less than perfect sense.

The observance of Labor Day falls on our calendars in September. Labor Day is a time to celebrate the workforce in America. It is a blessing to be able to work; to have a job that helps us support our families and live lives in this great big, beautiful world.

Likewise, Labor Day can provide us with a reason to celebrate remembering whose world this is and that we are not only able to live in this world but, as children of God, we get to live in God's heaven after we leave here. That realization helps us delight in our work here, knowing that, by sustaining ourselves and making this world better for having lived in it, we are furthering God's plan. As Paul said:

> *Whatever you do, work at it with all your heart, as working for the Lord, not for human masters* (Colossians 3:23).

September

Asters and Morning Glories

The word aster comes from the Greek word for "star." The aster flower is the shape of a star. But not just a 5-pointed star. The aster resembles a lush, brilliant star. And there was no more brilliant star than the one that shone over Bethlehem during Jesus' birth.

In ancient times, folks believed that burning the leaves of the aster flower would drive away serpents. In Christianity, the serpent represents Satan. And biblically, Christ stomped his heel on the serpent and conquered Satan.

Additionally, the aster is a symbol of love, faith, wisdom, patience and light. Coincidently, Jesus is love, faith, wisdom, patience and light.

The morning glory is a second birth flower for September. Its name refers to the fact that it that blooms in the morning. It thus reminds us of that glorious morning on Easter Sunday when Jesus' empty grave proved His power over death.

Because of its large saucer shape, the morning glory allows bees to pollinate it easily. As a result, new flowers bloom each day. Morning glories are therefore a powerful symbol of resurrection and new life.

> *"I am the resurrection and the life. The one who believes in me will live, even though they die"* (John 11:25).

September

The morning glory also grows in vines. It reminds us that Jesus said:

> *"I am the vine; you are the branches. If you remain in me and I in you, you will bear much fruit; apart from me you can do nothing. If you do not remain in me, you are like a branch that is thrown away and withers; such branches are picked up, thrown into the fire and burned. If you remain in me and my words remain in you, ask whatever you wish, and it will be done for you. This is to my Father's glory, that you bear much fruit, showing yourselves to be my disciples"* (John 15:5-8).

It is fitting for the month of September, that the primary birth flower is the aster. Asters are traditionally placed on graves as a symbol of remembrance. This is especially poignant in the United States as we remember the citizens who died on September 11, 2001.

And as the morning glory reminds us of Jesus' promise of eternal life, this second September birth flower gives us hope for us still living that one day we will live in glory with Him.

September

Sapphires

The birthstone for September is the sapphire. The diamond is the only mineral harder than the sapphire. That means you can wear sapphires every day, without having to worry about them cracking, being scratched or disintegrating.

According to folklore, the sapphire protects the wearer from evil and grants the wearer peace and joy. Its traditional blue color symbolizes truth, sincerity, and faithfulness, which is one reason women in many countries prefer a sapphire engagement ring.

Even better, Jesus protects us from evil and grants us His peace and joy. Jesus is truth and sincerity and is ever-faithful.

Medieval clergy wore sapphires to symbolize heaven, while commoners thought the gem attracted heavenly blessings. The sapphire's various shades of blue reflect the sky at different times of the day and night—from soft blue to twilight to midnight blue. Some ancient myths claimed our earth sat inside a large blue sapphire heaven.

Sapphires come in other colors than blue, however. In fact, the sapphire and the ruby are both in the same family of minerals—the corundum. The existence of additional mineral elements (such as iron, titanium, vanadium, chrome) in corundum, determine its ultimate color. When corundum contains chrome, it is called "ruby." All other colors of corundum are called "sapphires" and come in white (clear),

September

black, yellow, pink, green, blue, and violet—basically the colors of the rainbow.

Speaking of rainbows...God created them as a reminder to us and to Him of His love for us. One more way sapphires remind us of Jesus.

The sapphire is the state gemstone of Montana.

Need a Birthday Cake?

September traditionally marks the beginning of the school year. The best school lunches in the history of school lunches include peanut butter—either in sandwich or cookie form. Here's one more option.

Peanut-y Butter Cake

1 box yellow cake mix
1-1/4 cup milk
½ cup creamy peanut butter
1/3 cup oil
3 eggs

1 tub of prepared chocolate frosting

September

Mix together until smooth. Pour into 2 8 or 9-inch round cake pans, greased and floured. Bake at 350 (325 for dark or nonstick pans) for 30-35 minutes. Cool.

Peanut Butter Frosting

3 cups powdered sugar
8 ounce softened cream cheese
1 stick softened butter
½ cup creamy peanut butter

Whip together.

To assemble: Fill and frost cake layers as usual or alternate layers with your favorite chocolate frosting or a prepared one.

Sprinkle with chopped chocolate peanut butter cups, peanuts, chocolate sprinkles or chocolate and/or peanut butter chips, as desired.

Sharing Jesus with Others

Who do you know who has a birthday in September?

What about the month of September, asters, morning glories or sapphires would be of interest to that person?

How can you use that information to introduce them to Jesus?

What can you pray about for this person right now?

September

PRAYER: Heavenly Father, thank you for the people born in september. Thank you also for the great variety and excessive beauty you have filled this world with. Please help us see the beauty around us and be reminded that it is but a small reflection of your glory. Amen.

October: Marigolds, Tourmaline, Opal & Saints

~

Why, you do not even know what will happen tomorrow. What is your life? You are a mist that appears for a little while and then vanishes (James 4:14).

Let's Talk About October

The Latin prefix *oct* means eight. October was the eighth month in the Roman calendar before July and August were added. The numerical name was kept despite the fact that the month was no longer number eight. And, yes, you're going to hear a similar explanation about November and December.

October also features Halloween—a time for pumpkins and popcorn; trick-or-treat and tooth decay. But it began as a holy day.

October

A "saint" in Christianity refers to a believer. That's so for all varieties of Christianity, whether you are Roman Catholic, Orthodox or Protestant. A saint isn't just those martyrs holding a title of Saint with a capital "S."

All Christians—living and dead—are saints. Not because we're so good, but because we have been made holy through the blood of Christ. Sometimes in Scripture the word is translated as "holy people" or "God's people." But saints we are.

Back in the fourth century, merely 300 years after Jesus, the Roman Catholic Church established "All Saints Day," a holy day (holiday) on November 1 to recognize martyrs who had died for their faith. November first ultimately became a time to praise God for His plan of salvation and to remember all of Christ's saints (not just the ones with the capital "S") who had died and gone to heaven.

But what's Halloween?

Christians celebrate the evening before Christmas as Christmas Eve. Similarly, early Christians celebrated the evening before All Saints Day, referring to it as All Hallows Eve. "Hallowed," as we know from the Lord's Prayer, means "holy." This pre-All Saints Day observance gradually became known as "Hallows Eve" and eventually "Halloween." The meaning? Holy Evening.

Admittedly, there is nothing holy about passels of 4-foot tall aliens, fairy princesses and zombies roaming our neighborhoods with bulging bags of candy. And admittedly, the true evil one has a party every year as he encourages us to look to him for the glory, rather than to the true master of the universe.

But the fact that Satan uses a holy day for his purposes does not mean the day itself is evil. Does not the evil one use every day for his purposes? It is our responsibility as children of God to remember the holiness in everything—including and maybe even especially—days originally set aside by man for God's glory, such as Halloween.

Marigolds

The flower for the month of October is the marigold. Early Christians called the marigold flower, "Mary's Gold," reminding us of Jesus' earthly mother and that Jesus was God's precious gift to humanity.

The name of the flower also reminds us of the three gifts the Wise Men brought when they came to worship Jesus: gold, frankincense and myrrh. The marigold flower has therefore come to symbolize sacred affection.

The marigold's golden color, often tipped with rust, reminds us of a late-harvest, a time of year which still contains the last warmth of summer. Harvest itself reminds us of God's harvest of souls, through Jesus.

October

Tourmaline and Opals

There are two birthstones for the month of October—tourmaline and opal. Tourmaline comes in a variety of colors. More interestingly, tourmaline often has several colors in the same gemstone. The watermelon tourmaline is a great example. It is banded in green, white and pink colors. In gemstone symbolism, the three colors in watermelon tourmaline bring together compassion and emotional and spiritual love.

Wearing pink tourmaline supposedly brings out a person's inner child. Since Jesus reminds us that the kingdom of heaven belongs to the little children (Matthew 19:14), maybe we should wear pink tourmaline every day.

The more common birthstone for October is the opal. The name opal comes from the Greek word *opallos*, meaning "to see a change of color." Opals range in color from milky white to black and often contain flashes of yellow, orange, red, green and blue.

Opals are formed when silica gel seeps into the sedimentary strata of rock and hardens. As a result of this process, opals contain a high amount of water—up to 10% of the total weight of the stone. Thus, opals are both a stone and water—just as Jesus is referred to as our cornerstone and also the living water.

What is unique about both tourmaline and opal is that they both frequently display several colors in the same stone. It's as if each stone contains its own little rainbow—God's promise to us and to Himself after the flood. That promise was fulfilled through Jesus who came to save us and provide a way for us to live with Him in heaven.

Tourmaline is the state gemstone of Maine. Black fire opal is the state gemstone of Nevada.

Need a birthday cake?

Fall is the perfect time for a hearty Dutch apple cake. Think German Chocolate cake with apples. Extra moist. Extra good.

Dutch Apple Cake

Prepare a boxed fudge cake mix according to the package directions. Before baking, stir in 1 can apple pie filling, cut up slightly. Bake as directed in two 8 or 9-inch round pans.

Fill with chocolate frosting; top with the second layer. Frost sides of cake with chocolate frosting. Top with coconut pecan frosting.

October

Coconut Pecan Frosting

1 small can evaporated milk
3 egg yolks
1 teaspoon vanilla
1 cup sugar
½ cup margarine

Cook over medium heat until thick, stirring—about 12 minutes. Add 1-1/3 cup coconut and 1 cup chopped pecans. Stir briskly until thick. Spread on top of cake only.

Sharing Jesus with Others

Who do you know who has a birthday in October?

What about the month of October, marigolds, tourmaline or opal would be of interest to that person?

How can you use that information to introduce them to Jesus?

What can you pray about for this person right now?

October

PRAYER: Heavenly Father, thank you for the people born in October. Help us to remember you, Jesus, whenever we see a marigold, tourmaline or opals, and to thank you for becoming human for our sake. Amen.

November: Chrysanthemums, Topaz, Citrine & Sonshine

But encourage one another daily, as long as it is called "Today," so that none of you may be hardened by sin's deceitfulness (Hebrews 3:13).

Let's Talk About November

The Latin prefix *nov* means nine. November was the ninth month in the old 10-month Roman calendar. Since that no longer has any real meaning to us, it's nice that our month of November also contains Thanksgiving—a day to be thankful.

Thanksgiving Day falls on the fourth Thursday of November. Thus it moves across the calendar from one year to the next. Fortunately, every day is a day of thanksgiving when we remember what Jesus has done for us.

> *Do not be anxious about anything, but in every situation, by prayer and petition, with thanksgiving, present your requests to God. And the peace of God, which transcends all understanding, will guard your hearts and your minds in Christ Jesus* (Philippians 4:5-7).

In other words, whatever we go through, we have Jesus with us. We can nearly always find something good to be thankful for in every situation. If there simply is nothing we see, we can be thankful that God has a plan and it is good. We can be thankful that He has provided for our ultimate future with Him. We can be thankful that the Holy Spirit is going through life with us, strengthening us and being our friend.

The Chrysanthemum

The chrysanthemum is a member of the daisy family. Remember plucking the petals from a daisy and singing: "He loves me. He loves me not"? With Jesus, the answer is always, "He loves me."

The chrysanthemum was first cultivated in China 15 centuries before Christ as a flowering herb. The flowers can be boiled to make a sweet tea. According to eastern medicine, drinking this tea improves blood flow, reduces varicose veins and treats influenza. Tea or no tea, Jesus is the Great Physician, both for our physical health and our spiritual well-being.

November

The chrysanthemum was originally golden in color. It became a symbol of the sun. Jesus is not the "sun," but the Son. The chrysanthemum flower symbolizes long life, joy, optimism and fidelity. In Japan, the chrysanthemum's orderly petals represent perfection. Like Jesus.

Yellow Topaz and Citrine

The two birthstones for the month of November are yellow topaz and citrine. Both of these golden gemstones are the color of sunshine. Yellow topaz is naturally occurring; yet rare. Golden citrine is also rare in its natural state. Most commercial citrine today started out as purple quartz (amethyst) or smoky quartz and was turned golden by applying heat.

Ancient Egyptians believed that natural yellow topaz got its color literally from the sun; or rather from the rays of the sun god, Ra. Romans similarly affiliated topaz with Jupiter—who was the Roman god of the sun.

Ecclesiastes tells us though that there is nothing new under the sun. In other words, there is nothing new down here on earth. Above the sun, in heaven, is another story because above the sun—as well as in our hearts—is where Jesus resides.

Topaz is a symbol of wisdom, friendship, love, honesty, faithfulness, tenderness and purity. Sound anything like the fruit of the Spirit?

November

> *But the fruit of the Spirit is love, joy, peace, forbearance, kindness, goodness, faithfulness, gentleness and self-control* (Galatians 5:22-23).

Citrine is said to bring the wearer health, hope, energy and warmth. In ancient times, citrine was worn as protection against snakes and evil thoughts. A gift of citrine is symbolic of hope and strength. Jesus is our only hope of heaven and our sure strength for all trials.

Yellow topaz and citrine beautifully represent their month—at least for the Northern Hemisphere. Both gemstones are the color of harvest—the color of leaves after the first frost-cold night; of persimmon cookies, pumpkin pie and butternut squash. Both stones capture the warm glow of autumn and bring sunshine to the first days of the long winter to come.

As a reminder of harvest, yellow topaz and citrine point to the eternal harvest Jesus will begin when He returns. That harvest of souls. The one you and I are so eager to be part of.

> *Don't you have a saying, 'It's still four months until harvest'? I tell you, open your eyes and look at the fields! They are ripe for harvest* (John 4:35).

Topaz is the state gemstone of Utah.

November

Need a Birthday Cake?

The obvious choice for a November cake is pumpkin. And with a luscious cream cheese frosting, it's delicious any time of the year.

Plumpin' Pumpkin Cake

1 (15 ounce) can pureed pumpkin
2 cups sugar
1 cup oil
4 eggs
2 cups flour
2 teaspoons baking soda
1 teaspoon ground cinnamon
½ teaspoon salt

In bowl, beat pumpkin, sugar, and oil. Add eggs, and mix well. Add dry ingredients and beat until blended. Pour batter into two greased and floured 8-inch round pans. Bake at 350 degrees for 25 to 30 minutes. Cool and frost.

November

Cream Cheese Frosting

1 (8 ounce) package softened cream cheese
5 T softened butter
1-3/4 cup powdered sugar
3 teaspoons milk
1 cup chopped walnuts

In bowl, beat cream cheese, butter or margarine, and vanilla until smooth. Add 1 3/4 cups confectioners' sugar, and mix well. Add milk and mix again. Frost tops of cake only and sprinkle with nuts. OR make 2 recipes of frosting and also frost sides.

Sharing Jesus with Others

Who do you know who has a birthday in November?

What about the month of November, chrysanthemum, yellow topaz or citrine would be of interest to that person?

How can you use that information to introduce them to Jesus?

What can you pray about for this person right now?

November

PRAYER: Heavenly Father, thank you for the people born in November. Thank you also for seasons; for the reminder of the warmth of summer and the coolness of autumn during November. Thank you for harvest time on earth that reminds us that those of us who call upon your name are assured to be part of the eternal harvest to come. Amen.

December: Poinsettias, Blue Topaz, Tanzanite & Treasures

∼

For I know the plans I have for you," declares the Lord, "plans to prosper you and not to harm you, plans to give you hope and a future" (Jeremiah 29:11).

Let's Talk About December

The Latin prefix *dec* means ten. In the early Roman calendar, December was the tenth month. Now the month that means ten is the twelfth month of the year.

In addition to being the very last month of the year, when we can celebrate a year well lived, we can also look forward to new beginnings, another opportunity to do things better, a renewal of commitments. Those opportunities for new beginnings arrive with the brand new year to come.

December

Even better is that in December we have set aside a time to celebrate Jesus' earthly birth. No one knows the exact date of Jesus' birth. Most scholars agree that it probably was not December 25 or the Jewish equivalent of that date. But the exact date doesn't matter in the eternal scheme of things.

What does matter is that we have an opportunity to celebrate God's amazing plan of redemption that shook humanity for the better when Jesus was born in that little town of Bethlehem over 2,000 years ago.

In our society, folks sometimes despair that stores bring out Christmas decorations even before Halloween. But be of good cheer. Having Christmas decorations in the store provides us Jesus followers with the perfect opportunity to remind others of what Christmas is all about.

Early store decorations give us an opportunity to talk about Jesus, not just on Christmas day, but for an additional two or three months every year. We can twist our thinking to the positive and be thankful.

The Poinsettia

If you've been to the Caribbean, Hawaii, Mexico or Central America you may have seen enormous poinsettia bushes growing wild. The red of these tropical plants are actually leaves. The flower itself is tiny and located in the center of the leaves.

December

Aztecs believed the poinsettia was a symbol of purity. In modern times, it became a symbol of celebration, reassurance and joy. All of which epitomize Jesus.

Today, the poinsettia is the number one, best-selling potted plant in America. Nearly all of the plants are sold in November and December. Because of the flower's brilliant red and vibrant green colors, the poinsettia is an almost universal symbol of Christmas. And Christmas, of course, is all about Jesus.

One of the most famous flower legends is about the poinsettia. It says that on one Christmas Eve, the church in a small village held a special evening service. Attendees were to bring gifts in honor of baby Jesus. A young girl wanted to attend the service, but she was poor and had nothing to bring. Rather than dishonor Jesus by not attending the worship service, she picked some weeds alongside the road and humbly laid the bouquet on the altar.

The modest gift was pleasing to God because it had come from the heart of a child in true worship. In delight, God caused the weeds to blossom into brilliant red flowers.

This story reminds us of what Jesus said about our faith:

> *"Truly I tell you, unless you change and become like little children, you will never enter the kingdom of heaven"* (Matthew 18:3).

In other words, our worship should come from our heart.

December

Blue Topaz and Tanzanite

The birthstones for the month of December are the blue topaz and tanzanite. Blue topaz and tanzanite are popular gemstones used often in women's jewelry. But did you know that nearly all of the two gems found in their natural state begin as dull, brownish stones?

In fact, the exquisite tanzanite—found at the base of Mt. Kilimanjaro in Tanzania in 1967 and nowhere else on earth—was not recognized as a gemstone until a wildfire heated some of the brown stones on the ground and turned them the rich purplish blue color we know today. It was heat that did it. And heat is also routinely applied to natural brownish topaz to turn that gemstone blue.

Our souls, too—in their natural state—are dull and brownish; filled with unrepentant sin. We need Jesus to clean us up and make us sparkle.

Scripture tells us that Jesus will make us white as snow. When we think of laundry back in Grandma's day, we remember that she added bluing to the white load of laundry. A couple of squirts of blue liquid into the wash cleaned up Grandma's white clothes even better. She knew that blue white was even whiter than white.

So, too can Jesus clean up our souls so that they are whiter than white. Sometimes though, He has to do so by allowing us to go through fire.

December

> *This third I will put into the fire; I will refine them like silver and test them like gold. They will call on my name and I will answer them; I will say, 'They are my people,' and they will say, 'The Lord is our God"* (Zechariah 13:9).

And check out this Scripture that combines both a refiner's fire and a laundry reference:

> *But who can endure the day of his coming? Who can stand when he appears? For he will be like a refiner's fire or a launderer's soap* (Malachi 3:1-3).

In other words, God can transform our drab, brown souls into something that glorifies Him. He can turn them into something that reflects His glory.

There's one more way the blue topaz and blue/violet tanzanite perfectly reflect their birth month of December. The color we humans most generally associate with baby boys? Blue. Appropriate because during this month of December, we celebrate the human birth of the most precious baby boy in the history of humanity—Jesus Emanuel. God with us.

Blue topaz is the state gemstone of Texas.

Need a Birthday Cake?

This white cake with cranberry and orange is especially beautiful this time of year. If you don't know anyone who has a birthday to celebrate in this month, make it for Jesus, light a candle for Him and say a prayer when you blow it out. It just might become one of your new favorite Christmas traditions.

Christmas Cake for Jesus

Bake 2 white cake layers according to package instructions.

Prepare the filling/topping and frosting and assemble.

Filling and Topping

1 (12-oz.) jar cherry preserves
3/4 cup sugar
1/4 cup fresh orange juice
3-1/2 cups fresh or frozen (thawed) cranberries

In sauce pan, boil all ingredients, stirring for 5 until cranberries begin to pop. Cool 1 hour; then cover and chill 8 hours.

December

Orange Cream Cheese Frosting

1 cup butter, softened
1 (8-oz.) package cream cheese, softened
1/4 teaspoon salt
1 (32-oz.) package powdered sugar
2 tablespoons orange juice
1 teaspoon vanilla extract

Beat butter, cream cheese and salt with mixer until creamy. Gradually add powdered sugar, orange juice and vanilla. Beat at low speed until smooth.

To assemble:

Set 1 cake layer on a serving platter. Spoon 1 1/2 cups buttercream into a zip-top plastic freezer bag. Pipe a ring of frosting around cake layer just inside the top edge to keep filling in. Spread half the filling (without whole berries to the edge of frosting. Top with second cake layer. Spread remaining buttercream over top and sides of cake. Spread cranberry topping over top cake layer, spreading to edge.

Mix remaining filling and topping together and serve on the side—because folks will probably want a dab more. It's that good. Or save and pour over vanilla ice cream later.

December

Sharing Jesus with Others

Who do you know who has a birthday in December?

What about the month of December, the poinsettia, blue topaz or tanzanite would be of interest to that person?

How can you use that information to introduce them to Jesus?

What can you pray about for this person right now?

PRAYER: Heavenly Father, thank you for the people born in December. Thank you especially, Jesus for leaving heaven and being born here on earth. Thank you for everything that reminds us of Christmas and your love for us. Amen.

For Those Seeking Salvation

This little book is about finding Jesus. In actuality, He can be found everywhere if only we look. Sometimes though, it can be helpful to have new ways to share Jesus in normal conversations, without feeling like it must focus on theology, doctrine or require power point presentations and colored markers.

Scripture reminds us that even the stones cry out to honor King Jesus (Luke 19:40). Everything in nature praises God. Everything in nature reflects God's glory. Everything was made by His hand.

If we can see Jesus everywhere we look; if we look with the expectation of seeing Him, it's another way of walking with Him daily.

We, too were made by God's hand. We too reflect His glory—or should do so. Unlike the flowers of the field and rocks of the earth, God gave us the free will to squelch the glory He set inside us. But it is there—a light of glory—ready to be unveiled to light our way and shine a light to others, reflecting God's glory and letting others see a little bit of Jesus in us.

Jesus commands us to tell others about Him. He doesn't command us to save others, because we can't. Only Jesus can do that. All we can do is introduce Jesus to others and leave the saving up to Him.

If you have not yet accepted Christ as your Savior, why not do so now? Or maybe you know someone who needs Jesus. Jesus is right there waiting for all to come to Him. He died for all of mankind. Personally, He died for me and He died for you, too.

The theology behind Christianity can sometimes be daunting. But the first thing to do for understanding is to just believe—and then allow God to reveal whatever truth in whatever timing He determines you are ready to understand. It's what I did in my own spiritual journey. I read about the man who spoke to Jesus, saying:

I believe; help my unbelief! (Mark 9:24)

Then I prayed the "Salvation Prayer" (to follow) and simply asked God to answer my questions in His timing. He surely is doing that!

I had tried for years to understand every aspect of Christianity completely before surrendering my life to Jesus. I wanted all the answers before I took that step. I had determined to understand every aspect of established Christian doctrine before I committed my life to it.

That's what I had wrong. Being a Christian is not about committing to an established doctrine. It is about committing to Christ. And then allowing Him to work in our lives so that we live our lives like Christ lived His.

So when I read about the man in Mark, I saw a truth. I can believe and then let the one who *is* truth reveal His truth to me more and more as I am able to understand.

We may not have all of the answers to our questions about God's plan in this lifetime. But we don't need to have all of the answers to be saved. We simply and only need to receive the gift of God's forgiveness and His accompanying grace and mercy that Jesus provided through His death on the cross.

Salvation begins in our hearts by turning our hearts toward the one who loves us most. Christian lingo calls this first step, "saying the Salvation Prayer." You can pray any way you like, but a salvation prayer generally consists of three parts:

- Acknowledge in your heart that Jesus is Lord and confess it with your mouth.

- Believe that Jesus died for your sins.

- Repent of (turn away from) your sins and give control of your life to Jesus.

Here's a simple salvation prayer. You can pray this yourself or use it to lead someone who wants to accept Jesus. Then watch as God proves His plan and character to you!

For Those Seeking Salvation

Dear Jesus, I admit I am a sinner. I am sorry. I turn away from my sins and ask you to forgive me. I believe you died on the cross to save me, you rose from the grave and are alive right now. I receive you as my Savior and ask you to take control of my life. Thank you for forgiving me and giving me eternal life. Help me to live every day in a way that pleases you. Amen.

If you or someone you know struggles with the letting go of self and surrendering to Jesus, the most logical "argument" is this:

1. If a person believes in Jesus and lives his life in a way that honors God, if God does in fact exist, that person spends eternity in heaven. If that believer dies and it turns out that God does not exist, then that person is simply gone forever. But he has lived a good life, following principles that make his life better. And he has left behind a legacy of love.

2. On the other hand, consider an atheist who dies. If it turns out that God does not exist, being right about the "God" question is of no value. There is be no eternal reward for being an atheist and being right.

3. If, on the other hand, an atheist dies and finds out he was wrong, he will be judged. Because Jesus did not know him in life, the person will have no one to stand up on his behalf before the throne of judgment. Perfect heaven has no room for an unforgiven sinner. The only option

for that person who did not have Jesus in life, is eternity in hell.

For a person using his rational mind, it's a no-brainer. Choose Jesus. If you're wrong and there's no heaven; no hell; no God; no anything, then you've lost nothing by living your life as if there is.

But if you reject Jesus and it turns out that Jesus is the only way to live forever in heaven, you've lost everything. Forever.

Choose everything. And then watch God prove Himself to you.

Keep Finding and Sharing Jesus

Here's a short summary of the information in this book. You can use it as a reference when thinking of what to share with people about finding Jesus in the months of the year. Maybe it will help you find a focus for what you'd like to share with others.

JANUARY: Named for Roman god Janus, the god of gates. Jesus is the narrow gate. No one can enter heaven except through Him. Carnations symbolize mother's love. The word *corone* means to crown the king, reminding us of King Jesus; the word *carnis* meaning flesh reminds us of God made flesh in Jesus. The red garnet reminds us of Jesus' blood shed for us; symbolizes eternal friendship and trust; believed to protect a person from evil—only Jesus can do that.

FEBRUARY: Named for Roman festival of water purification. Jesus is the living water to wash us clean spiritually and satisfy our spiritual thirst. St. Valentine reminds us of love; Jesus is the true author and giver of love and died to prove it. The iris' sword-shaped leaves remind us that the Word of God is the sword and that Jesus Himself is the Word. Violets and irises represent faith and hope which we have in Jesus. Amethyst symbolizes heavenly understanding, spiritual contentment and unity of mind, body and spirit and is one of the 12 foundations of heaven. Purple symbolizes royalty, reminding us of King Jesus.

MARCH: Named for Mars, the Roman god of war. Warrior Jesus battles Satan for our souls. Daffodils symbolize rebirth, resurrection and friendship, reminding us of our friend Jesus, His resurrection and that we are spiritually reborn through Him. Aquamarine reminds us that Jesus is the living water. It is said to help us connect with heaven.

APRIL: Named for Aphrodite the Greek goddess of love. God so loved the world that He sent His only Son to die for us. Sweet peas and daises symbolize happiness, innocence and certainty. Jesus, our source of joy purifies us and gives us assurance of our salvation. Diamonds represent faithfulness, love, purity and eternity—all characteristics of Jesus.

MAY: Named after Maia, the Roman goddess of spring, whose name means "great one." Only our God is great. Mother's Day reminds us of Jesus' earthly mother Mary's advice: "Do whatever Jesus tells you." Lilies of the Valley remind us that God takes care of even the lilies and that Jesus was called a lily of the valleys. Emeralds symbolize rebirth. The Emerald is associated with the Roman goddess of love. Our God is the true God of love.

JUNE: Named after Juno, the Roman goddess of marriage. June is a popular month for weddings in our society, reminding us that we, the Church, seek to remain faithful to Jesus until He returns to take us home as His spiritual bride. Roses are sturdy and strong. The thorns remind us of the character flaws God is working on and remind us of the crown of thorns Jesus wore at His crucifixion. Pearls are symbols of the Gospel, which should be our number one priority. Pearls protect the oyster; only God can protect us from evil. The gates of heaven are made of pearls.

JULY: Named after Julius Caesar. We celebrate political freedom on July 4. Every day we celebrate our freedom from sin because Jesus died for us on the cross. Larkspurs have blossoms of 5-pointed stars, pointing us to Jesus. The water lily reminds us that Jesus is the living water and symbolize sacred enlightenment, purity and divine birth. Red rubies remind us of Jesus' blood. Scripture says godly wisdom and a noble character are more precious than rubies.

AUGUST: Named for Augustus Caesar. The first Sunday of August is both Friendship Day and International Forgiveness Day. Jesus, our friend, died to forgive our sins. The gladiolus (sword lily) is named for gladiators. If they lost in battle, they were cast into a pit. Jesus, who battles Satan for our souls, rescued us from the spiritual pit. The poppy symbolizes gentleness, which balances the warrior flower, the gladiola. Peridot was believed to have the power to drive away evil. The stone was in the High Priest's breastplate and is part of the foundation of heaven.

SEPTEMBER: The prefix *sept* means seven, referring to the seventh month of the calendar before the Caesars added 2 months to the calendar. Seven is the number of perfection and is referred to as God's number. Labor Day reminds us to work as for God, being His hands and feet, accomplishing His will in this world. The word aster means "star," reminding us of the one that shone over Jesus' birth. Asters symbolize love, faith, wisdom, patience and light. The morning glory symbolizes resurrection and new life, its vine reminding us that Jesus is the vine, we are the branches and that we can do nothing without Him. Sapphires are said to protect against evil and grant peace, joy and heavenly blessing. They symbolize truth, sincerity and faithfulness.

OCTOBER: The prefix *oct* means eight which made sense when it was the eighth month in the 10-month calendar. The name Halloween was shortened from "All Hallows Eve," the evening before All Saints Day, an early church holy day to honor God's people. Marigolds were also called "Mary's Gold," reminding us of Jesus' mother and the gift of the Wise Men. Tourmaline and opal often contain more than one color in the same gemstone, reminding us of God's promise in the rainbow. Opals contain water, meaning that they are both a stone and water; just as Jesus is our cornerstone as well as living water.

NOVEMBER: The prefix *nov* means nine which made sense when it was the ninth month in the 10-month calendar. It is the month that contains Thanksgiving. Scripture reminds us to be thankful in all circumstances. Chrysanthemums symbolize long life, joy, optimism, faithfulness and perfection. Egyptians and Romans associated yellow topaz and citrine with their sun gods. Solomon said there is nothing new under the sun. Fortunately, above the sun, in heaven, is where God resides.

Topaz symbolizes wisdom, friendship, love, honesty, faithfulness, tenderness and purity. Citrine brings health, hope, energy and warmth and wards off evil thoughts.

DECEMBER: The prefix *dec* means ten which made sense when it was the tenth month in the 10-month calendar. As the last month of the year we can celebrate a year well lived and look forward to new beginnings. The poinsettia is the best-selling potted plant in America. The legend of the poinsettia reminds us to worship God with the heart of a child. Most blue topaz and tanzanite begin as dull, brown stones. When heated, they turn sparkling blue. Jesus turns our souls sparkling clean when we turn to Him. Blue is the color we associate with baby boys, reminding us that Jesus's birth is celebrated in December.

Who I might share Jesus with and their birthdays:

JANUARY:

FEBRUARY:

Keep Finding and Sharing Jesus

MARCH:

APRIL:

MAY:

JUNE:

JULY:

Keep Finding and Sharing Jesus

AUGUST:

SEPTEMBER:

OCTOBER:

NOVEMBER:

DECEMBER:

More Flowers, Gemstones, Gold & Silver in Scripture

Additional Scripture about Flowers

The life of mortals is like grass, they flourish like a flower of the field; the wind blows over it and it is gone, and its place remembers it no more (Psalm 103:15-16).

The desert and the parched land will be glad; the wilderness will rejoice and blossom. Like the crocus, it will burst into bloom; it will rejoice greatly and shout for joy (Isaiah 35:1-2).

The grass withers and the flowers fall, but the word of our God endures forever (Isaiah 40:8).

"And why do you worry about clothes? See how the flowers of the field grow. They do not labor or spin. Yet I tell you that not even Solomon in all his splendor was dressed like one of these. If that is how God clothes the grass of the field, which is here today and tomorrow is thrown into the fire, will he not much more clothe you—you of little faith?" (Matthew 6:28-30).

"Consider how the wild flowers grow. They do not labor or spin. Yet I tell you, not even Solomon in all his splendor was dressed like one of these. If that is how God clothes the grass of the field, which is here today, and tomorrow is thrown into the fire, how much more will he clothe you—you of little faith! (Luke 12:27-28).

But the rich should take pride in their humiliation—since they will pass away like a wild flower. For the sun rises with scorching heat and withers the plant; its blossom falls and its beauty is destroyed. In the same way, the rich will fade away even while they go about their business (James 1:10-11).

Additional Scripture about Gemstones

When he came near the place where the road goes down the Mount of Olives, the whole crowd of disciples began joyfully to praise God in loud voices for all the miracles they had seen:

"Blessed is the king who comes in the name of the Lord!"

"Peace in heaven and glory in the highest!"

Some of the Pharisees in the crowd said to Jesus, "Teacher, rebuke your disciples!"

"I tell you," he replied, "if they keep quiet, the stones will cry out" (Luke 19:37-40).

All who were willing, men and women alike, came and brought gold jewelry of all kinds: brooches, earrings, rings and ornaments. They all presented their gold as a wave offering to the Lord (Exodus 35:22).

Gold there is, and rubies in abundance, but lips that speak knowledge are a rare jewel (Proverbs 20:15).

More Scripture

A wife of noble character who can find? She is worth far more than rubies (Proverbs 31:10).

"Afflicted city, lashed by storms and not comforted, I will rebuild you with stones of turquoise, your foundations with lapis lazuli. I will make your battlements of rubies, your gates of sparkling jewels, and all your walls of precious stones (Isaiah 54:11-12).

I adorned you [Jerusalem] with jewelry: I put bracelets on your arms and a necklace around your neck, 12 and I put a ring on your nose, earrings on your ears and a beautiful crown on your head. 13 So you were adorned with gold and silver; your clothes were of fine linen and costly fabric and embroidered cloth. Your food was honey, olive oil and the finest flour. You became very beautiful and rose to be a queen (Ezekiel 16:11-13, explanation added).

You were in Eden, the garden of God; every precious stone adorned you: carnelian, chrysolite and emerald, topaz, onyx and jasper, lapis lazuli, turquoise and beryl. Your settings and mountings were made of gold; on the day you were created they were prepared (Ezekiel 28:13).

The Lord their God will save his people on that day as a shepherd saves his flock. They will sparkle in his land like jewels in a crown (Zechariah 9:16).

At once I was in the Spirit, and there before me was a throne in heaven with someone sitting on it. And the one who sat there had the appearance of jasper and ruby. A rainbow that shone like an emerald encircled the throne (Revelation 4:2-3).

It [Jerusalem] shone with the glory of God, and its brilliance was like that of a very precious jewel, like a jasper, clear as crystal (Revelation 21:11, explanation added).

The wall was made of jasper, and the city of pure gold, as pure as glass. The foundations of the city walls were decorated with every kind of precious stone. The first foundation was jasper, the second sapphire, the third agate, the fourth emerald, the fifth onyx, the sixth ruby, the seventh chrysolite, the eighth beryl, the ninth topaz, the tenth turquoise, the eleventh jacinth, and the twelfth amethyst. The twelve gates were twelve pearls, each gate made of a single pearl.

> *The great street of the city was of gold, as pure as transparent glass* (Revelation 21:18-21).

Additional Scripture about Precious Metals

Exodus and Numbers contain many verses about covering the holy items in the Tabernacle with gold and silver. See also 1 Kings, 2 Kings, 1 Chronicles and 2 Chronicles about gold and silver items in the building of the Temple by King Solomon.

> *If you return to the Almighty, you will be restored: If you remove wickedness far from your tent and assign your nuggets to the dust, your gold of Ophir to the rocks in the ravines, then the Almighty will be your gold, the choicest silver for you* (Job 22:23-25).

> *But he knows the way that I take; when he has tested me, I will come forth as gold* (Job 23:10).

> *And the words of the Lord are flawless, like silver purified in a crucible, like gold refined seven times* (Psalm 12:6).

> *The fear of the Lord is pure, enduring forever. The decrees of the Lord are firm, and all of them*

are righteous. They are more precious than gold, than much pure gold; they are sweeter than honey, than honey from the honeycomb (Psalm 19:9-10).

I love your commands more than gold, more than pure gold (Psalm 119:127).

My fruit is better than fine gold; what I yield surpasses choice silver (Proverbs 8:19).

How much better to get wisdom than gold, to get insight rather than silver! (Proverbs 16:16).

The crucible for silver and the furnace for gold, but the Lord tests the heart (Proverbs 17:3).

Remove the dross from the silver, and a silversmith can produce a vessel (Proverbs 25:4).

Like apples of gold in settings of silver is a ruling rightly given (Proverbs 25:11).

More Scripture

The crucible for silver and the furnace for gold, but people are tested by their praise (Proverbs 27:11).

"The silver is mine and the gold is mine,' declares the Lord Almighty (Haggai 2:8).

Surely the islands look to me; in the lead are the ships of Tarshish, bringing your children from afar, with their silver and gold, to the honor of the Lord your God, the Holy One of Israel, for he has endowed you with splendor (Isaiah 60:9).

How the gold has lost its luster, the fine gold become dull! The sacred gems are scattered at every street corner (Lamentations 4:1).

By your wisdom and understanding you have gained wealth for yourself and amassed gold and silver in your treasuries (Ezekiel 28:4).

This third I will put into the fire; I will refine them like silver and test them like gold. They will call on my name and I will answer them; I will say, 'They are my people,' and they will say, 'The Lord is our God.'" (Zechariah 13:9).

More Scripture

*Then Peter said, "Silver or gold I do not have, but what I do have I give you. In the name of Jesus Christ of Nazareth, walk." * (Acts 3:6).

If anyone builds on this foundation using gold, silver, costly stones, wood, hay or straw, 13 their work will be shown for what it is, because the Day will bring it to light. It will be revealed with fire, and the fire will test the quality of each person's work (1 Corinthians 3:12-13).

These have come so that the proven genuineness of your faith—of greater worth than gold, which perishes even though refined by fire—may result in praise, glory and honor when Jesus Christ is revealed (1 Peter 1:7).

Your beauty should not come from outward adornment, such as elaborate hairstyles and the wearing of gold jewelry or fine clothes. 4 Rather, it should be that of your inner self, the unfading beauty of a gentle and quiet spirit, which is of great worth in God's sight (1 Peter 3:3).

Author's Thanks

Thank you for reading this book. If you like what you've read, please consider leaving a word or two for other readers who might enjoy this book also at Amazon.com.

Please go to my website www.carolpetersonauthor.com for more ways to pray for others and for articles on faith.

Books by Carol Peterson

From Honor Bound Books

With Faith Like Hers Bible Study Series: Studies on the character and circumstances of women in Scripture. Books include:

> *I am Eve*
> *I am Esther*
> *I am Ruth*
> *I am Mary*
> *I am Elizabeth*
> *I am Rahab*

Flowers, Gemstones & Jesus: Finding Jesus in the Months of the Year

The Praying Writer: Prayers for the Writing Process

Wielding the Sword: Inductive Bible Study. Because The Bible is Even Better When You Know What it Says (Kindle only)

From Libraries Unlimited

Fun with Finance: Math + Literacy = $uccess (2009)

Jump into Science: Themed Science Fairs (2007)

Around the World Through Holidays: Cross-Curricular Readers Theatre (2005)

Jump Back in Time: A Living History Resource (2004)

About the Author

Carol writes to inspire, educate and entertain. Her focus is sharing God's love with the world through a study of Scripture and opening other's eyes to see evidence of Jesus in the world around them.

She lives in Idaho with her husband of almost 40 years, leads women's Bible studies and tries to keep up with the ideas the Holy Spirit tosses her way for "just one more book...or seven."

You can find Carol online at her website where she posts about faith: www.CarolPetersonAuthor.com.

www.ingramcontent.com/pod-product-compliance
Lightning Source LLC
Chambersburg PA
CBHW070459100426
42743CB00010B/1688